DATE DUE			

LIFE DURING THE GREAT CIVILIZATIONS

The Mongol Empire

Don Nardo

BLACKBIRCH PRESS

An imprint of Thomson Gale, a part of The Thomson Corporation

THOMSON
★
GALE

Detroit • New York • San Francisco • San Diego • New Haven, Conn. • Waterville, Maine • London • Munich

For more information, contact
Blackbirch Press
27500 Drake Rd.
Farmington Hills, MI 48331-3535
Or you can visit our Internet site at http://www.gale.com

LIBRARY OF CONGRESS CATALOGING-IN-PUBLICATION DATA

Nardo, Don, 1947–
  The Mongol empire / by Don Nardo.
    p. cm. — (Life during the great civilizations)
  Audience: Grades 7-8.
  Includes bibliographical references.
  ISBN 1-4103-0585-6 (hard cover : alk. paper)
  1. Mongols—History—To 1500—Juvenile literature. I. Title. II. Series.
DS19.N37 2005
950'.2—dc22
                                             2005010418

Printed in United States
10 9 8 7 6 5 4 3

Contents

The Largest Empire in History

In the year 1219, Bukhara, a city in central Asia, suffered death and devastation on a terrible scale. Seemingly out of nowhere, an army of mounted warriors appeared and attacked. The intruders slaughtered most of the town's 30,000 citizens and burned their homes. The few hundred survivors were herded into a church, and the leader of the attackers mounted the pulpit to address them. "O people," he said, "know that you have committed great sins." The proof for this charge was simple, he told them. "I am the punishment of God. If you had not committed great sins, God would not have sent a punishment like me upon you."[1]

The man who repeated these words often and became famous for them was Genghis Khan, ruler of the Mongols.

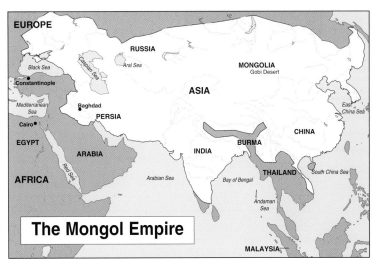

The Mongol Empire

Opposite Page: This statue of Genghis Khan, the ruler of the fearsome Mongols, stands in the town of Elista in Russia.

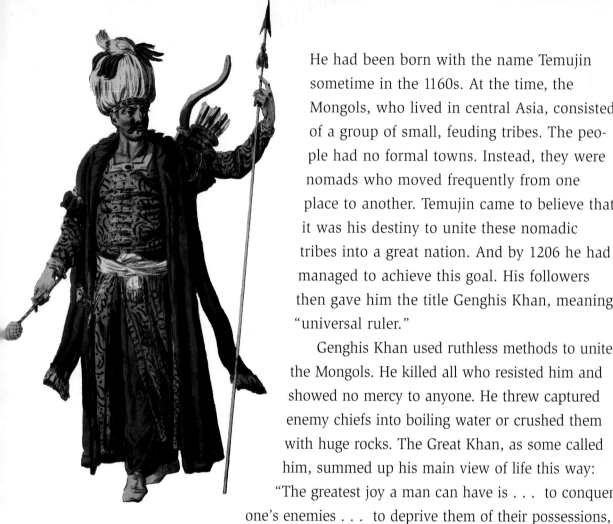

He had been born with the name Temujin sometime in the 1160s. At the time, the Mongols, who lived in central Asia, consisted of a group of small, feuding tribes. The people had no formal towns. Instead, they were nomads who moved frequently from one place to another. Temujin came to believe that it was his destiny to unite these nomadic tribes into a great nation. And by 1206 he had managed to achieve this goal. His followers then gave him the title Genghis Khan, meaning "universal ruler."

Genghis Khan used ruthless methods to unite the Mongols. He killed all who resisted him and showed no mercy to anyone. He threw captured enemy chiefs into boiling water or crushed them with huge rocks. The Great Khan, as some called him, summed up his main view of life this way: "The greatest joy a man can have is . . . to conquer one's enemies . . . to deprive them of their possessions, [and] to reduce their families to tears."[2]

Above: An 18th-century portrait by a French artist shows Genghis Khan prepared for battle. Opposite page: A 16th-century illustration shows Genghis Khan's Mongol army storming a fortress in western China.

Genghis Khan and his Mongols used this same warlike creed to justify conquering other peoples. In the decades that followed, they swept across the Asian plains, or steppes. City after city suffered the same fate as Bukhara. The Mongols burned the great city of Kiev (in modern-day Ukraine) to the ground, and they totally destroyed the splendid city of Baghdad (in modern-day Iraq). The invaders also overran China, Korea, Poland, and many other lands. At its height, in the mid- to late 1200s, the Mongol Empire was the largest the world had ever seen. It spanned almost all of Asia.

Even though it was immense, the great Mongol realm did not last long. After its founder's death, it broke up into several smaller kingdoms. These kingdoms fought one another, which weakened them. Also, more and more Mongols settled in towns and adopted the locals' customs. Over time this caused many of the Mongols' traditional customs and beliefs to disappear. By the late 1300s, the Mongol threat to the world was over.

CHAPTER ONE

The Nomadic Lifestyle

The society into which Temujin, later called Genghis Khan, was born was a nomadic one. Individual Mongol groups moved often from place to place on the vast Asian steppes. In many cases, these migrations were motivated by the need to graze horses, cattle, and other livestock in fertile areas. Sometimes a Mongol group stayed in one place for a year or two or more. But the makeshift dwellings always formed a temporary camp rather than a town. And when the people inevitably moved on, they packed up all their belongings, leaving nothing behind.

Families, Clans, and Tribes

In addition to being nomadic, Mongol society was tribal and clannish. The individual Mongol tribes were fairly small. Each consisted of only a few thousand people. They were also not united and often quarreled among themselves. There was no overall leader until Temujin brought people from many different tribes together under his rule.

Usually even each separate Mongol tribe, or irgen, had no leader. Instead, tribal affairs were guided by a council made up of clan leaders. Each tribe consisted of several clans. A typical clan, or obok, was a large kinship group made up of several families. The clan leader, or batur, led the group's warriors in wartime. In peacetime, however, he had less say in clan decisions, including when to pack up and move and where to set up

A modern Mongolian family migrates with its flock of sheep through Mongolia's Dorhad Valley.

a new camp. Such decisions were made largely by a meeting of the heads of individual families, who were always men.

Mongol families were very large by modern standards. A Mongol man was allowed to have several wives, and each wife had several children. In addition, a family often included grandparents and in-laws. So it was not unusual for the members of a single family to number in the dozens. This made family life complicated in some ways. For example, there was not enough room for everyone in a single house. So one family might reside in two, three, or more houses.

Temporary, Portable Dwellings

Because of the Mongols' nomadic lifestyle, these houses were both temporary and portable. Yet they were also quite sturdy. A typical house, called a ger, and later a yurt, was about 16 feet (5m) in diameter. It was essentially a big tent, with layers of felt stretched across a wooden frame. The felt was made of compressed layers of sheep's wool. To make the felt waterproof, people smeared it with animal fat. William of Rubruck, a 13th-century European monk who visited the Mongol Empire, added: "Frequently they coat the

A man in the deserts of Mongolia stands outside his yurt, a hut made of wood and wool.

This Mongolian nomad is pounding sheep's wool into layers of felt that he will use for the walls of his yurt.

felt with chalk, or white clay, or powdered bone, to make it appear whiter."[3]

Inside the ger, the owners made a floor by laying down wooden planks and covering them with felt. They left an open space in the middle. There they built a simple stone hearth for cooking and heating. The smoke from the fire exited through a hole in the middle of the roof.

When it was time to move the camp, the family members dismantled the house and loaded everything onto large wooden carts drawn by teams of oxen. Sometimes they did not even bother to take a house apart. William saw a family place a completely intact house on a huge cart:

I myself once measured the width between the wheel tracks of a cart [as] twenty feet, and when the house was on the cart, it projected beyond the wheels on either side [by] five feet at least. I have myself counted to one cart twenty-two oxen drawing one house. . . . The axle of the cart was as large as the mast of a ship.[4]

Clothes and Food

Among the belongings carried by the carts were extra clothes. Both men and women wore woolen trousers. Over these pants they wore a sacklike garment made of wool or leather. The women's version was decorated with small pleats and tucks, while the men's version was plain. Warm clothing was a must because the Asian steppes can be windy and cool, even in summer. In the winter, it sometimes gets brutally cold, so practically everyone had felt or fur coats and hats. They also wore woolen or leather boots, which they lined with fur in the winter.

The wool, leather, and other materials used to make clothes came from the livestock the Mongols raised. In addition to horses and cattle, these included sheep and goats. Similarly, most of the foods the Mongols ate came from these animals. In fact, their diet consisted almost entirely of dairy products and meat. The only grain they consumed was millet, which they boiled to make a breakfast dish similar to oatmeal. Another staple food was a white alcoholic drink made from mare's milk called kumiss. They also used milk to make various kinds of cheese.

Typical Mongol dress consisted of clothes and hats made from wool, leather, and fur.

Although the Mongols ate meat, they preferred to slaughter their livestock only when necessary. So they often waited until an animal died naturally. "If it happens that an ox or a horse dies," William recalled, "they dry its flesh by cutting it into narrow strips and hanging it in the sun and wind [to dry]. With the intestines of horses they make sausages."[5]

Such use of the intestines stemmed in part from the belief that it was wrong to waste any part of an animal. Along with the flesh, hides, and fur, the Mongols ate or made clothes or other items from almost every body part. They even chewed and sucked the marrow from animal bones. William described a leather bag, called a captargac, "in which they store away bones when they have not time to

Women Workers and Warriors

In his *Story of the Mongols* (translated into English by Helga and Stuart Drummond), the 13th-century Italian monk Giovanni Carpini described the wide range of skills possessed by Mongol women:

Mongol women, like this young modern Mongolian woman, were known for their skill in riding horses.

The girls and women gallop on their horses just as skillfully as the men. We also saw them carrying bows and quivers. Both men and women can stay in the saddle for a long time. . . . All work rests on the shoulders of the women. They make fur coats, clothes, shoes . . . and everything else made from leather. They also drive the carts and mend them, load the [pack animals], and are very quick and efficient in all their work. All women wear trousers, and some of them shoot with the bow as accurately as the men.

gnaw them well, so that they can gnaw them later and that nothing of the food is lost."[6]

The Important Roles of Women

Cooking and other preparation of these animal products was strictly women's work. Other jobs done almost solely by women were caring for children, making clothes, repairing the ger, and packing belongings and loading them on the travel carts. In contrast, men fought, hunted, made and mended weapons and saddles, and constructed the travel carts.

One of the most important duties expected of Mongol women was to get married. According to social custom, a bride could not be a member of her husband's tribe. So sometimes a boy's parents met with the parents of a girl from another tribe and arranged the marriage. Other times men stole or bought girls from rival tribes. Once a man had taken several wives, he usually picked a favorite and spent more time with her than the others. Giovanni Carpini, an Italian monk who was a contemporary of William of Rubruck, was surprised that multiple wives "do not readily quarrel among themselves."[7]

Carpini was also surprised to see that Mongol women could ride horses and shoot bows as well as men. These skills helped to ensure the survival of clans and tribes. Because Mongol groups were often on the move, they frequently faced new and unexpected dangers. And everyone—whether male or female—had to be ready on a moment's notice to defend the camp.

CHAPTER TWO

Religious Beliefs and Practices

Despite their murderous attacks on, and lack of mercy for, their enemies, the Mongols were no less spiritual than other medieval peoples. However, traditional Mongol beliefs and worship were very different than those of Christianity, Judaism, Islam, and Buddhism. These faiths, which the Mongols encountered during their conquests, were more organized and formal. They had sacred holy writings, such as the Bible and Koran, which contained moral codes or guidelines. They also had churches, mosques, and other formal places of worship.

In contrast, the traditional Mongol faith had no holy writings, formal moral codes, or churches. Nor did the Mongols believe in a single, all-powerful God, as the Christians, Jews, and Muslims did. Instead, the Mongol religion combined aspects of two very ancient religious systems. These were animism and shamanism, both of which date back to the Stone Age in many parts of the world. According to animism, formless spirits exist throughout nature. These spirits inhabit both living and nonliving things such as rocks, trees, and water.

Peoples who believed in animism usually practiced shamanism as well. A shaman, which the Mongols called a kam, was a sort of medicine man or wizard. More properly, he was a spirit guide. The Mongols believed that, through visions and dreams, shamans could reveal the will of the spirits. It was also believed that a kam could predict important

Opposite Page: In this 16th-century illustration, Genghis Khan and his army pray to nature spirits before going into battle.

happenings, such as eclipses of the Sun. In addition, William of Rubruck observed that "they predict lucky and unlucky days for the undertaking of all affairs. And so it is that they [the Mongols] never assemble an army nor begin a war without the assent [of a shaman]."[8]

Nature Alive with Spirits

The spirits whose will the Mongol shamans interpreted were seemingly unlimited in number. Some were thought to exist naturally in various animals and objects. Others were the spirits of deceased humans. Ancestor worship was a crucial part of Mongol religion, and each house had a small shrine on the north side of the hearth to honor the family's dead.

A Mongol shaman dances during a ritual to honor the spirits of the dead.

More powerful than these minor spirits was an almighty spirit named Mongke Koko Tengri, or Tengri for short. His name meant "eternal blue sky." Christian and Muslim observers assumed that Tengri was similar to the all-powerful creator God whom they worshipped. However, the Mongols believed that Tengri was a formless universal force that existed in all things and kept nature in balance. Another important Mongol spirit was Nachigai. Mistress of grass, crops, and herds, she was a sort of earth goddess or Mother Nature figure.

The Mongols believed that human affairs and activities sometimes threatened to upset the balance of nature. Tengri, Nachigai, and other spirits wanted that balance to be maintained. And they possessed the power to punish those who threatened to harm the natural order. The Mongols also believed that Tengri and other spirits would punish people for showing disrespect to the spirits. Such punishment might take the form of a drought, leaving humans and animals without water. Or the spirits might keep hunters from catching game.

Prayers and Offerings

Hoping to avoid divine punishment and maintain the goodwill of the spirits, the Mongols worshipped these spirits on a regular basis. The main forms, or rituals, of worship were prayer and sacrifice. Often people prayed to little statues called ongols which represented various spirits. Those that stood for human spirits were fashioned in human form. During his visit to the steppes, Giovanni Carpini saw these statues and wrote:

An engraving shows Genghis Khan trying to learn his destiny from a shaman.

> They have certain idols made out of felt in the shape of human figures, which they set up on both sides of the entrance to the yurt. Beneath these idols they put some felt figures which look like a [cow's] udder [representing Nachigai], and which they believe [will, when prayed to,] protect their herds and provide them with an abundance of milk.[9]

Not all Mongol prayer was directed at statues. A surviving Mongol work describes Genghis Khan praying to the spirit of a tall and imposing mountain. The khan removed his belt and hat, which were symbols of his earthly authority. Then he "struck his hand into his breast, and, kneeling nine times toward the sun, offered . . . a prayer."[10]

The other form of worship, sacrifice, consisted of offering something of worth to a spirit or spirits. Most often the offering consisted of food and drink, especially meat and mare's milk. In the case of milk, it was common to toss some into the air. The belief was that the spirit being worshipped took whatever nourishment it wanted from the liquid and left the rest. Carpini reported that the Mongols also offered animals, including horses, to the spirits.

Dressed as a Mongol warrior, a Mongolian man beats his drum during a religious ceremony.

Sin and Purification

Carpini also commented on certain striking Mongol practices relating to the concepts of sin and purification of sin. Although the Mongols lacked holy books containing religious laws, he said, they did have strong traditions about sin. In their view, sins were actions that interfered with, or insulted, the spirits of nature. For example, because fire was thought to be inhabited by a potent spirit, it was a sin to poke a knife into a fire. Similarly, Carpini said:

> It is a sin to lean on the whip with which they beat horses . . . to touch arrows with the whip, to catch or kill young birds . . . to break one bone with the help of another . . . or to urinate inside a tent. Anybody who does so intentionally pays for it with his life.[11]

Fire also played a part in purifying, or cleansing, sin. When a man died, it was considered wise to purify all his belong-

ings. This was done to make sure that any sins he may have committed had not tainted the objects. Someone purified the objects by carrying them between two fires. In a like manner, foreigners wishing to see a Mongol leader had to walk between two fires. It was hoped that this would erase any evil intent they might have.

Religious Toleration

One thing that foreigners found remarkable about the Mongol faith was its toleration for other belief systems. The Mongols did not try to convert people to their faith or force their beliefs on anyone. In fact, Genghis Khan granted complete religious freedom to all conquered

Whose Priests Are More Powerful?

In 1275 twenty-year-old Marco Polo accompanied his father, Niccolo, a Venetian merchant, on a trip to Asia. It was Niccolo's second visit to the court of Kublai Khan, grandson of Genghis Khan. In his later account of his travels, Marco told how the elder Polo had earlier observed the remarkable religious toleration of the Mongols. In fact, the khan was very friendly toward Christians. Why then, Niccolo had asked, did the Mongol leader not convert to Christianity? Kublai Khan answered that he had seen Buddhist monks make drinking cups float through the air. But no Christian priests had been able to perform such miraculous feats. The khan challenged Polo to have the pope send 100 priests. If they could perform miracles and convert the Buddhists, then he would agree to convert to Christianity. As it turned out, the pope never sent the priests and Kublai Khan never converted.

These woodcut medallions show the busts of Marco Polo and Kublai Khan.

peoples. And he even gave tax exemptions to their churches, mosques, and temples.

These policies were based partly on the fact that the Mongols worshipped multiple spirits. They seem to have assumed that other peoples worshipped one or another of these same spirits but simply called them by different names. There was also a political motive for tolerating other faiths. When treated well, religious leaders in conquered lands helped Mongol rulers maintain control over local populations. Thus, the Mongol faith was a strange mix of old and new. It combined spirit worship as old as humanity itself with a degree of religious toleration that would not be seen again until modern times.

CHAPTER THREE

The Khan's Great Law Code

Foreigners who visited the Mongol Empire in the 13th and 14th centuries were almost always surprised. Like everyone else, they had heard frightening stories about the Mongols. These tales told how the warriors of the steppes were cruel, uncivilized murderers. They had no morals and no concept of, or respect for, law and order or justice. Yet, the visitors discovered that the Mongols did have a system of laws and justice. In fact, that system was codified, or written down. It was also evenly applied to everyone, regardless of wealth, and usually strictly enforced.

Mongol laws and justice were collectively called yasa. The written Mongol law code, the Great Yasa, was compiled by Genghis Khan between 1206, the year he united the tribes, and 1218. No complete copy has survived. But substantial fragments exist in the works of foreigners who observed Mongol society up close.

Application of Law and Justice

The Great Khan knew that making laws was one thing and applying and enforcing them was another. The Mongols had been used to dealing with justice on the local, tribal level. But this small-scale, fairly simple approach was no longer possible. The growing empire encompassed vast territories and millions of people. The Mongols needed an administrative system that governed a large realm and allowed for applying the yasa to everyone far and wide.

Opposite Page: The Mongol army demands the surrender of the ruler of Bokhara, a city in what is now Russia.

MARCVS POLVS

During his travels, Venetian explorer Marco Polo visited Genghis Khan's grandson, Kublai Khan.

Genghis Khan set up just such a system. The Venetian traveler Marco Polo, who visited the khan's grandson, Kublai Khan, described it. Polo said that the realm's thirty-four provinces were administered by twelve governors. Each province had

a presiding law officer, together with several clerks, who have their . . . apartments in the court, and there [they] transact whatever business is necessary to be done for the province to which they belong.[12]

These law officers, or judges, applied justice evenly to all, regardless of the social status of the person accused of wrongdoing. Similarly, visiting foreigners were no less bound by the laws. William of Rubruck recorded an incident that occurred when he and his traveling companions were visiting Mongke Khan, another of Genghis Khan's grandsons. Through an interpreter, Mongol attendants told the Europeans about a law against touching the threshold of the house of a Mongol war leader. William and his friends were careful not to touch the threshold when they entered. But on the way out, one of the visitors accidentally brushed against it. "Those who were guarding the threshold," William wrote, "laid hands on my companion, stopped him and would not allow him to follow us. [They took] him to . . . the grand secretary of the court, who condemns persons to death."[13]

The subsequent fate of William's friend shows that Mongol justice could be fair as well as strict. William protested to the judge, saying that the interpreter had not made the letter of the law clear enough. On this technical point, the judge allowed the prisoner to go free. Similarly, some Mongol laws were astonishingly fair and tolerant by medieval standards. One law provided complete toleration for foreign religious beliefs and declared that priests and scholars did not have to pay taxes.

Laws Reflect Mongol Customs and Morality

Most Mongol laws, however, dealt with the Mongols themselves. Often these rules were based on ancient tribal customs. So they reveal valuable

Marco Polo and Kublai Khan are shown riding in the khan's elephant car during the explorer's visit to China.

Justice Tempered with Mercy

Though Mongol justice was often harsh, individual Mongol leaders sometimes showed mercy if they felt the circumstances warranted it. This is proven by an incident reported by the Persian historian Juvaini. Ogedei, son of Genghis Khan, condemned to death three men who had been convicted of a crime. A few minutes later, Ogedei came upon a sobbing woman and asked her what was wrong. She answered:

A Persian manuscript shows Genghis Khan with his three sons.

"Of those men whom you ordered to be put to death, one is my husband, another is my son, and the third my brother." "Choose one of them," said Ogedei, "and for your sake he shall be spared." "I can find a substitute for my husband," replied the woman, "and children, too, I can hope for; but for a brother there can be no substitute." Ogedei spared the lives of all three.

information about traditional Mongol life and ways. By non-Mongol standards, these customs and the laws governing them sometimes bordered on the bizarre. According to the Persian historian Juvaini, for example:

> It is laid down in the *yasa* (law) and custom of the Mongols that in the seasons of spring and summer no one may sit in water by day, nor wash his hands in a stream, nor draw water in gold or silver vessels, nor lay out washed garments on the plain, it being their belief that such actions increased the thunder and lightning.[14]

Some laws also reflected the Mongols' peculiar moral beliefs and practices. Like several other ancient and medieval peoples, for instance, they observed strict rules for slaughtering animals. A law stated that the animal's belly must be slit open and the heart squeezed until the beast died. The Mongols were horrified when they witnessed Muslims and others killing animals by slitting their throats. As a result, the law specifically forbade slaughter in the "Muslim fashion."

Other Mongol laws dealing with morality were strikingly similar to those in the holy writings of the Muslims, Jews, and Christians. It was forbidden to lie and to commit adultery, for example. One of Genghis Khan's laws said that one must love one's neighbor as one loves oneself and must not hurt a neighbor. Another law demanded that people show respect for elders and beggars.

Harsh Punishments

The punishments for breaking the laws established by the Great Khan were generally harsh. The death penalty was used for a wide range of crimes. Adulterers and thieves were put to death, for instance. Someone who urinated into water or ashes was executed, as was a person who touched the threshold of a commander's house or slaughtered an animal in the Muslim fashion. Using sorcery to harm someone was also punishable by death. And going bankrupt

Genghis Khan watches as a blindfolded prisoner is violently flogged.

three times resulted in a death sentence. For most offenders, execution methods were bloody. Hacking a person to death with swords was common. In contrast, persons of high military or social rank were allowed a less bloody end. They were stuffed inside a carpet and beaten to death.

Some offenses were punished by death only if the guilty person could or would not perform lesser penalties. Murder is a good example. A convicted murderer had the option of paying a heavy fine. But if he could not pay it, he was executed. A horse thief was ordered to return the stolen horse plus nine others of equal value. If he could not do so, his children were taken as substitutes for the horses. But if he had no children, he was put to death.

Conviction for most other crimes resulted in a severe beating with sticks or paying a heavy fine. Soldiers who neglected their duties or disobeyed an order were beaten. A hunter who allowed an animal to escape was also beaten.

By today's standards, Mongol justice seems overly harsh. But it was based on the hard realities of nomadic life on the bleak Asian steppes, and it served the Mongols well during the brief period in which their huge empire prospered.

CHAPTER FOUR

Military Skills and Innovations

The Mongols were a nomadic people who lived in tents on the open plains and cooked their food over open fires. They had no machines, electricity, or other types of technology that are taken for granted today. Or at least they had no machines in the sense of devices with mechanical parts, such as cars or radios. Some experts have argued, however, that the Mongols did have a sort of living machine. This was their extraordinary army. In this view, the soldiers' toughness, amazing riding and fighting skills, and superior organization and strategies all combined to operate like a well-oiled machine.

It was this military machine that allowed an otherwise technologically primitive people to create the largest empire in history. Marco Polo recognized this fact. In his famous travel journal, he wrote, "It is from these qualities, so essential to the foundation of [superior] soldiers, that they are fitted to subdue the world, as in fact they have done . . . to a considerable portion of it."[15]

Superior Toughness and Organization

The first quality of the Mongol military machine singled out by Polo was the remarkable efficiency of the individual Mongol soldier. Each fighting man, he said, was amazingly tough and disciplined. "When there is a necessity for it," Polo recalled, Mongol fighters "can march for ten days" without eating. During this period, "they subsist upon blood

---

Opposite Page: Kublai Khan and his army prepare
for battle from the security of a fortress carried
on the backs of three armored elephants.

drawn from their horses, each man opening a vein and drinking." In addition, Mongol troops could "remain on horseback during two days and two nights without dismounting." They often slept in the saddle while their horses grazed. "No people upon earth can surpass them in fortitude under difficulties,"[16] Polo said.

Polo was also impressed by the courage of Mongol soldiers. "They are brave in battle almost to desperation," he said. They seemed to place little value on their own lives, as they exposed themselves "without hesitation to all manner of danger."[17] Each fighter considered his own safety and survival to be secondary to that of the army as a whole.

Teamwork was therefore a key asset of Mongol armies. And excellent teamwork was achieved through highly efficient organization. The army was divided into units based on the decimal system, consisting of multiples of ten. The largest single unit, a tumen, was composed of 10,000 men. A tumen consisted of ten groups of 1,000 soldiers, each called a minghan, and the division continued with units of 100 and 10 men each. Each unit, whether large or small, had its own commander. Individual commanders strictly followed the orders of their superiors. This occurred all the way up the chain of command, ending at the top with the khan himself. This system ensured that every soldier in the army would follow a battle plan swiftly and precisely.

Masters of Stealth and Deception

As for the Mongols' battle plans, whenever possible they avoided engaging enemy forces head-on in hand-to-hand combat. Instead, their strategies usually involved some kind of stealth or deception. One of their favorite tactics, for example, was the feigned, or fake, retreat. A Mongol army would approach an enemy force as if planning to give battle. But then the Mongols would pretend to be afraid, turn, and run away. The fooled enemy troops almost always gave chase. At a preset

Great Respect for Horses

One of the keys to the Mongols' amazing military success was their skill in taming, training, and riding horses. In the 12th and 13th centuries, wild horses roamed the Asian steppes in herds up to 10,000 strong. When-ever possible, Mongol warriors captured young horses and trained them carefully for some years. These steeds could run fast, per-form sharp turns, and, like their owners, go for long peri-ods without food. The Mongols developed great respect, even love, for their horses. Genghis Khan set down strict rules that ensured the humane treatment of horses. Also, any horse that had been ridden in battle could not be killed for food or its hide.

In this woodcut, a Mongol warrior displays impressive horsemanship.

Dressed as a medieval Mongol archer, a modern Mongolian man demonstrates the power of the composite bow.

signal, the Mongols would suddenly turn around, ride to the sides, and try to surround their surprised opponents.

A variation of the feigned retreat was the feigned withdrawal. In this case, the Mongols fled completely out of their opponents' sight. Mistakenly thinking the Mongols were gone for good, the enemy broke ranks and made camp. Then, many hours later, seemingly out of nowhere, the Mongols would return and attack the camp.

The World's Most Effective Bow

When the Mongols finally attacked an enemy, they did so with an array of low-tech but effective weapons. Each Mongol warrior carried a sword or battle-ax and a lance. A lance was a spear a horseman used to stab at an opponent.

However, the Mongols much preferred to use their most lethal weapon—the composite bow. It was made of numerous materials that were combined in an innovative way. And this made it the closest thing to a technological device the Mongols possessed. Ordinary bows, or simple bows, are made from a single piece of wood. English longbows, used in the same period as the Mongol bows, are an example. In contrast, Mongol bows were made from one or more kinds of wood as well as animal horn and sinew (animal tendons). A Mongol warrior pieced these materials together using a very strong glue made by boiling fish bladders. The horn gave the bow extra strength. The sinew added extra springing power.

The result was the most effective bow ever devised before the 20th century. The English longbow, a very effective weapon in its day, could shoot an arrow up to 750 feet (228m). By comparison, a Mongol bow could shoot up to 1,050 feet (320m). Moreover, Mongol archers achieved amazing accuracy. Each man carried a wide assortment of arrows. Some, with metal tips, were for killing enemy fighters. Other arrows were designed to ignite fires or make a whistling sound for signaling.

The Mongols in Battle

The way the Mongols used these bows in battle was also innovative. When pretending to flee, for instance, they sometimes turned and fired backwards at the enemy. They also developed an amazing ability to time the release of an arrow with a horse's movements. An archer

A Mongol archer on horseback reaches into his quiver of arrows as his horse gallops along.

often fired during the split second when all four hooves were off the ground. That reduced the vibrations that might affect the accuracy of the shot.

Most often, the mounted Mongol archers fired their arrows from a distance. This was usually enough to defeat or scare away an enemy force. Only when a Mongol commander deemed it absolutely necessary did he order his troops to engage in close-in fighting. Marco Polo's account contains a vivid description of a real Mongol battle in which both of these tactics were employed:

Fierce Mongol warriors march in formation in a scene from the 2004 film, Genghis Khan.

> [A] signal, by the orders of the grand Khan, was first given to the right and left wings. And then a fierce and bloody conflict began. The air was instantly filled with a cloud of arrows that poured down on every side. . . . The loud cries and shouts of the men, together with the noise of the

horses and weapons, were such as to inspire terror. . . . When their arrows had been discharged, [they] engaged in close combat with their lances [and] swords. . . . Such was the slaughter, and so large were the heaps of [bodies] . . . that it became impossible for the one party to advance upon the other.[18]

In one battle like this one after another, the Mongols exploited their limited technology, cleverness, and fearlessness to the utmost. It is no wonder that they terrorized so many people and conquered much of the known world.

In this engraving, Mongol warriors cut the ears off the slain bodies of their enemies.

Notes

Introduction: The Largest Empire in History

1. Quoted in Ata-Malik Juvaini, *History of the World Conqueror*, trans. John A. Boyle., 2 vols. Manchester, England: Manchester University Press, 1958, vol. 1, p. 102.
2. Quoted in Fergus Fleming, ed., *The Mongol Conquests*. New York: Time-Life, 1989, p. 13.

Chapter 1: The Nomadic Lifestyle

3. Quoted in William W. Rockhill, ed. and trans., *The Journey of William Rubruck*. London: Hakluyt Society, 1909, p. 9.
4. Quoted in Rockhill, *The Journey of William Rubruck*, p. 9.
5. Quoted in Rockhill, *The Journey of William Rubruck*, p. 13.
6. Quoted in Rockhill, *The Journey of William Rubruck*, p. 14.
7. Giovanni Carpini, *The Story of the Mongols*, excerpted in Bertold Spuler, *History of the Mongols*, trans. Helga and Stuart Drummond. London: Routledge and Kegan Paul, 1972, p. 80.

Chapter 2: Religious Beliefs and Practices

8. Quoted in Rockhill, *The Journey of William Rubruck*, p. 142.
9. Carpini, *Story of the Mongols*, pp. 71–72.
10. Anonymous, *The Secret History of the Mongols*, trans. Francis W. Cleaves. Cambridge, MA: Harvard University Press, 1982, p. 37.
11. Carpini, *Story of the Mongols*, p. 74.

Chapter 3: The Khan's Great Law Code

12. Marco Polo, *A Description of the World*, published as *The Travels of Marco Polo*. New York: Orion, n.d., pp. 156–57.
13. Quoted in Rockhill, *The Journey of William Rubruck*, p. 97.
14. Juvaini, *History of the World Conqueror*, vol. 1, p. 204.

Chapter 4: Military Skills and Innovations

15. Polo, *Travels*, p. 87.
16. Polo, *Travels*, pp. 87, 89.
17. Polo, *Travels*, p. 87.
18. Polo, *Travels*, pp.113–14.

Glossary

animism: An ancient belief system that held that spirits inhabit everything in nature, including nonliving objects.

batur: A Mongol clan leader.

captargac: A leather bag used to carry bones and other items.

composite bow: A very powerful bow made by gluing together pieces of wood, animal horn, and sinew.

ger: A tentlike house that could be easily assembled or dismantled.

Great Yasa: The law code established by Genghis Khan between 1206 and 1218.

irgen: A Mongol tribe.

kam: A Mongol shaman.

kumiss: An alcoholic drink made by fermenting mare's milk.

lance: A spear used by a mounted horseman to poke or stab his opponents.

minghan: A Mongol army unit containing 1,000 men.

obok: A Mongol clan.

ongot: Small statues representing spirits.

shaman: A spirit guide or medicine man believed to possess the ability to interpret the will of various spirits or gods.

tumen: A Mongol army unit containing 10,000 men.

yasa: Mongol laws and justice.

For More Information

Books

Jennifer Hanson, *Mongolia*. New York: Facts On File, 2003.

Robert Nicholson, *The Mongols*. New York: Chelsea House, 1994.

Earle Rice, *Empire in the East: The Story of Genghis Khan.* Greensboro, NC: Morgan Reynolds, 2005.

Robert Taylor, *Life in Genghis Khan's Mongolia.* San Diego: Lucent, 2001.

Web Sites

The Mongols Bow (www.coldsiberia.org/monbow.htm). A very detailed examination of the chief technological accomplishment of the Mongols—their effective composite bow.

The Mongols (http://members.tripod.com/~ whitebard/ca54.htm). The home page for a group of links leading to informative articles about Mongol culture.

Women in Mongol Society (www.coldsiberia.org/monwomen.htm). A useful overview of the roles that women played in Mongol society. A link provides access to a long list of articles on a wide range of topics about the Mongols.

Index

Picture Credits

About the Author

Historian Don Nardo has published many volumes for young readers about ancient and medieval civilizations, including *The Roman Empire, A Travel Guide to Ancient Alexandria, The Etruscans, Empires of Mesopotamia, The Byzantine Empire, Life on a Medieval Pilgrimage,* and *Weapons and Warfare of the Middle Ages.* He lives in Massachusetts with his wife, Christine.